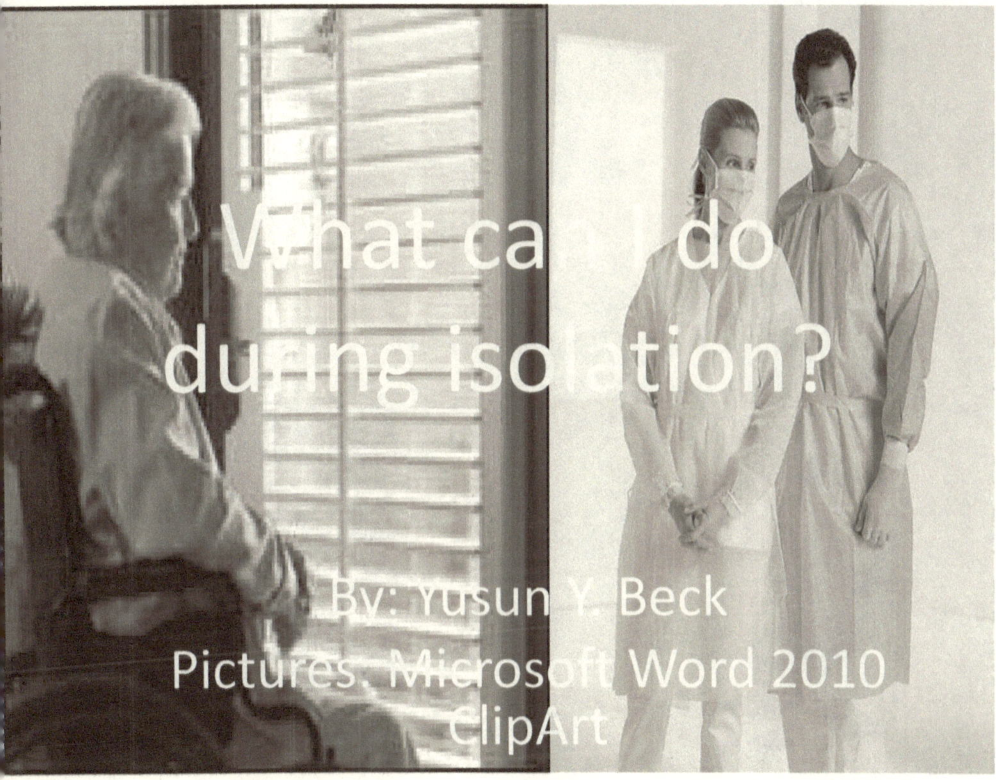

What can I do during isolation?

By: Yusun Y. Beck

Pictures: Microsoft Word 2010 ClipArt

What can I do during isolation?

Dedications

This book is written in dedication to all the healthcare professionals working on the frontlines. It is for all of the parents working to take care of children during the COVID-19 situation. It is to all the teachers trying to work together with administrators to build plans. It is a hope for everyone to hold hands "virtually" in the goal of working together and trying their best to do what is right for each other and their fellow man. People are hearing a lot about what they can't do. We can wash our hands. We can do other things too. We can be safe. We can be respectful. We can be responsible. We can show love. We can show grace. We can be honest. We can be helpful. We can use integrity, courage, and bravery. We can stand up and lead by choosing to do what is right and shine as beacons of light. We do this by remembering to love our neighbors as ourselves, and putting our best foot forward daily. I am thankful for everyone who is trying their absolute best to do this daily where the rubber meets the road. Always be strong and stay encouraged, for this too shall pass.

What is this child doing?

He is reading! That means I can ask for help from my mom or dad to read a book. I can read a book on my own.

What are they doing?
I can practice social distancing at six feet apart and play on electronics. Social distancing is six feet apart.

I wonder what he is doing?
He looks like he is practicing counting cans with materials in his cabinet.
That is amazing!

I hear you have been talking about balls!

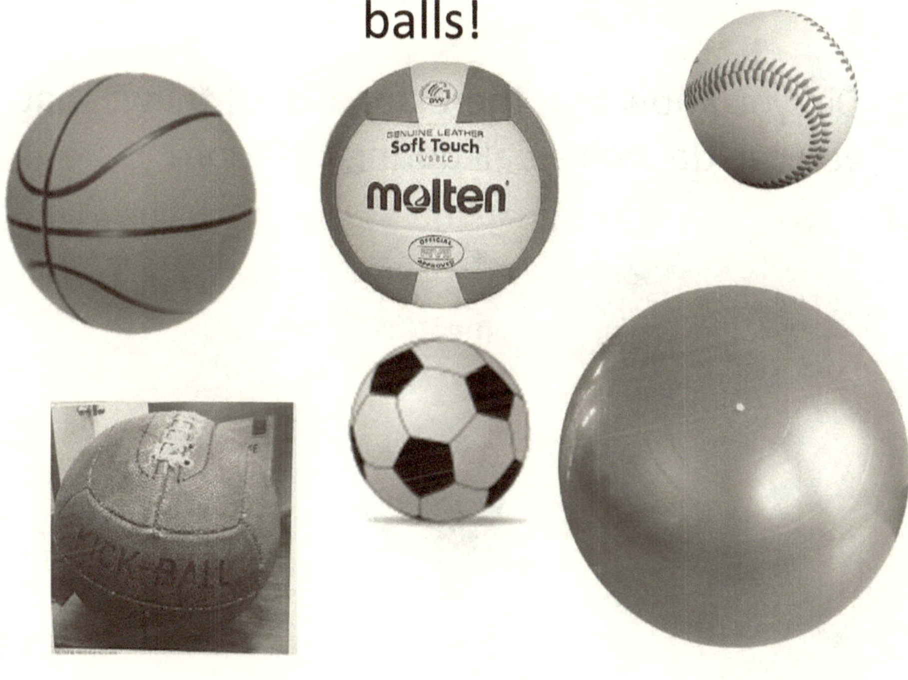

Balls are a lot of fun!

Did you know that there are a lot of things that you can do with a ball during isolation?

You can stretch and exercise on an exercise ball during isolation.

What can you do with a basketball by yourself?

You can practice dribbling, shooting, and throwing the basketball by yourself with or without a hoop if you have one at home or not. You don't need to go to the court to practice.

What can you do with a baseball?

You can practice throwing a baseball!

What can you do with a volleyball?

You can practice setting a volleyball!

What can you do with a soccer ball?

You can practice kicking a soccer ball in your backyard or by yourself.

What can I do with a kickball?

I can practice tossing a kickball. I can roll it. I can surely kick it with my parents!

Wow! I can practice new studies like Martial Arts too!

I learned that being by myself with just my parents allows me to learn new things. I can have lots of fun like painting. I don't have to be bored. Yeah! You can also do some things too. Let's have fun!

Special Thanks:

All of the people who are there helping others when they don't have to. Continue to be helpful.

Special Thanks:

- My Mother: Hazel Arango
- My Step Father: Jose Arango
- My Wife: Melissa Daignault
- My Close Friend: A Obest
- Many Others…

Special Thanks:

- My Brothers in Arms which there may be too many to list. I respect all of the veterans, servants of the public, and many community

Special Thanks: You are the heroes of tomorrow!